Adorable Kittens
Coloring Book

Adorable Kittens
Coloring Book

Snuggle down with these friendly fur pals

SIRIUS

SIRIUS

This edition published in 2024 by Sirius Publishing, a division of
Arcturus Publishing Limited,
26/27 Bickels Yard, 151–153 Bermondsey Street,
London SE1 3HA

Copyright © Arcturus Holdings Limited

All rights reserved. No part of this publication may be reproduced, stored in a
retrieval system, or transmitted, in any form or by any means, electronic,
mechanical, photocopying, recording or otherwise, without written permission in
accordance with the provisions of the Copyright Act 1956 (as amended). Any
person or persons who do any unauthorised act in relation to this publication may
be liable to criminal prosecution and civil claims for damages.

ISBN: 978-1-3988-4386-8
CH012197NT

Printed in China

Introduction

If you had to create the epitome of a cute baby animal, it might well look a lot like a kitten. Big ears, wide eyes, soft fur, and a cuddly body just bursting with playfulness make the delightful critters hard to beat as special companions and playmates. This new coloring book has more than 40 images of kittens doing the most kittenish things. So you'll find them chasing wool or butterflies, curled up to sleep in a fruit bowl, popping out of a teacup, or just snoozing in a pile with other kittens. There are super simple designs for you to color quickly and other, far more complex arrangements that will take more concentration to fill in. There are patchwork kittens and floral kittens, realistic kittens, and cartoon kittens. All you need to do is choose your favorite design, select your preferred medium, and get coloring to create a purrfect furry friend.

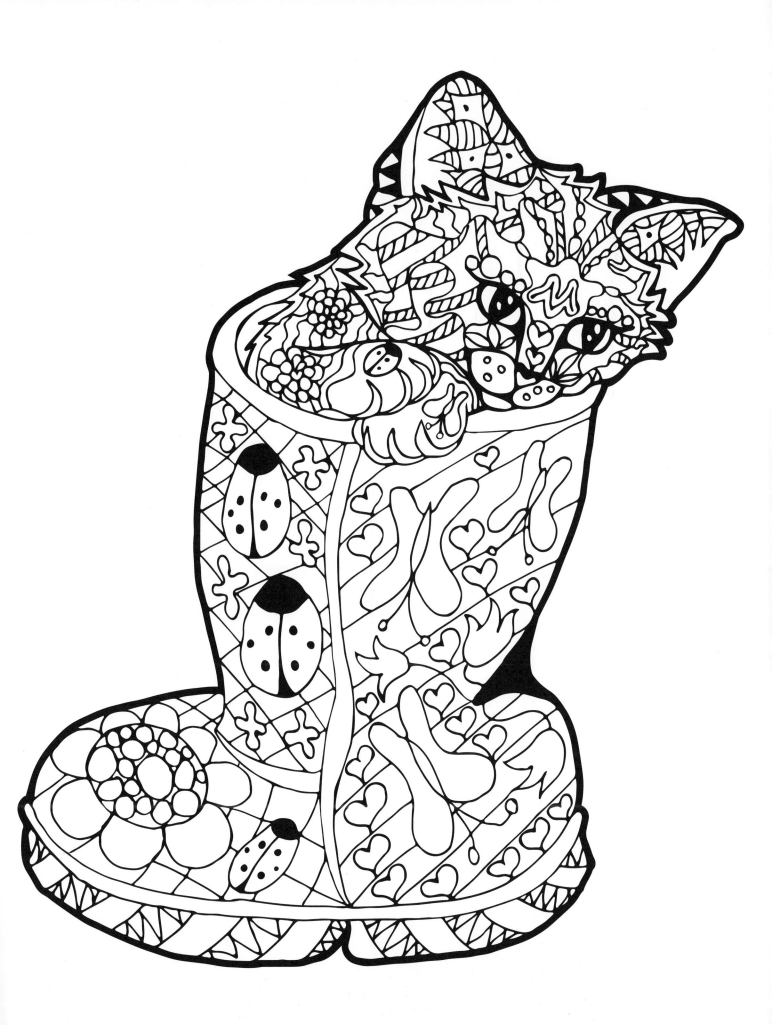